MASK OFF:

21 Days to Being *Mad* Free

MIKE MCCLURE, JR.

Scripture quotations taken from the New American Standard Bible® (NASB),
Copyright © 1960, 1962, 1963, 1968, 1971, 1972, 1973, 1975, 1977, 1995 by The Lockman Foundation. Used by permission. www.Lockman.org

Scripture quotations are taken from the Holy Bible, New Living Translation, copyright ©1996, 2004, 2007, 2013, 2015 by Tyndale House Foundation. Used by permission of Tyndale House Publishers, Inc., Carol Stream, Illinois 60188. All rights reserved.

Scripture quotations are taken from GOD'S WORD®, © 1995 God's Word to the Nations. Used by permission of Baker Publishing Group.

Scripture quotations are taken from THE MESSAGE, copyright © 1993, 1994, 1995, 1996, 2000, 2001, 2002 by Eugene H. Peterson. Used by permission of NavPress. All rights reserved. Represented by Tyndale House Publishers, Inc.

Printed in the United States of America

First Printing: July 2017

ISBN 978-0-692-93241-4

McClure Publishing
Birmingham, AL 35214

INTRODUCTION

Life is hard. This is an uncomfortable reality that we all must face at one point or another.

Chances are, you've been in some complex situations and relationships that left you feeling hurt, confused, and jaded, so much in fact that to protect yourself against future hurt, you've put up a barrier between you and everyone else. In other words, you're a mess…with a mask on.

You're not alone, however, because to some extent, we all are. But it's time to let go and realize you can be free of the mask and the madness that compels you to wear it. God created you to excel in every area. You owe it to Him and to yourself to live up to your fullest potential.

Over the next twenty-one days, we will not only focus on hearing from God, but also examining ourselves. We'll retrace our steps to determine where we took a wrong turn and chart a new course to get back on track.

Mask Off: 21 Days to Being Mad Free is a devotional inspired by the Madness Behind the

Mascara® conference. Each day features a scripture, quick lesson, and space to journal your thoughts. This isn't just another devotional written from one perspective. It's about you finding your voice and unpacking your journey.

Let the unmasking begin…

DAY 1: MASK OFF

"Let's take a good look at the way we're living
and reorder our lives under GOD."
Lamentations 3:40 (MSG)

---

*Life is too short to spend hoping that the
perfectly arched eyebrow or hottest new lip
shade will mask an ugly heart.* ~Kevyn Aucoin

As a woman, you are one of the most fascinating
creatures God ever created. Arguably, you're
the most prized thing a man can ever attain.

Simply put, you're bad and you know it. So bad
that Solomon said that "he who finds a wife
finds a good thing and obtains favor with the
Lord."

Say it with me, "I'm a *good thing*, I'm *blessed*,
I'm *favored*, and I'm...*FAKE!*

Sadly, many women have perfected the practice
of pretending.

Now, hold on a second. Before you chalk this book up as a waste of time and money, let me explain.

You are beautiful, however; you are probably the least likely to value how beautiful you really are.

As a result, you spend your time trying to create a flawless persona that is publicly appealing, but privately killing you. Inside, you're dying a slow, uncomfortable death because you feel crushed, defeated, and misunderstood. As I stated in my first book, *I Don't Like My Life:*

The Latin term for persona is stage mask. We essentially create these personas (on and offline), or wear these masks, to represent the best part of who we are, or who we want people to think we are, to protect our image or brand.

And this is important. If you're going to have a presence in the world, you should take care to put on the best possible performance. All the world's a stage, right?

The paradox is those masks make us feel safer even when they become suffocating.[1]

Here's what you must understand: Your blessing is in your authenticity. It is in you surrendering and submitting your life and being to God.

To start your journey to *Destination Mad Freedom*, ask yourself the following questions:

What masks do I wear? How do I allow others to define me?

_____

_____

_____

_____

_____

_____

_____

_____

_____

_____

_____

_____

_____

_____

_____

_____

_____

DAY 2: WHO ARE YOU?

"God has made us what we are. He has created us in Christ Jesus to live lives filled with good works that he has prepared for us to do."
Ephesians 2:10 (GW)

Never forget what you are, for surely the world will not. Make it your strength. Then it can never be your weakness. Armour yourself in it, and it will never be used to hurt you.
~George R.R. Martin

In life, we're trained and conditioned by our dominant influences, most often, by Mama and Daddy—what they did or didn't say, what they did or didn't do—shaped by their presence or troubled by their absence.

From childhood on, we're afflicted by unhealthy home-of-origin issues, but we learn to cope with them rather than deal with them, which results in a distorted sense of identity and self.

By the time we're adults, we're masters at masquerading. No one knows who we really are without the mask—not even us.

There are several disguises we might wear:

- **The Imposter** – This person fakes as if everything is okay. But in truth, her anxiety levels are so high that she is only one incident away from total collapse.

- **The Rebel** – The rebel acts as if nothing bothers her, but deep down, she longs for acceptance.

- **The Loser** – The loser acts as if she's helpless and wants everyone to do everything for her.

- **The Victim** – The victim acts as if everyone owes her something.

Do you ever find yourself slipping into one of these disguises?

If you do, don't trip. At times, we're all guilty of pretending like we're fine when we're not, and at any given moment, any one of the mindsets I've described might manifest when we least expect it.

Fortunately, and most importantly, however, masks are not permanent. We can swap out stifling disguises for a spirited disposition that serves us far better than those masks ever will.

From this day forward, consider yourself:

- **The Victor** – The victor is aware of her issues, but sees them as opportunities, not obstacles. She engages her problems with courage, confident that she'll find a solution and when she does, she knows that she will emerge stronger and better than she was before.

Today, make the choice to no longer be defined by a set of finite circumstances when you have complete access to an infinite God.

Think about today's verse...From the very beginning you were on God's mind. He has a plan for you, and He has something for you to do. The God who created the universe has something for you—yes, *you*—to do!

Spend some time today contemplating who you are, and use the next pages to describe how you feel with your mask on, and how you imagine you'd feel without it.

Who am I? What mask(s) do I wear? What would I look and feel like without it/them?

_____

_____

_____

_____

_____

_____

_____

_____

_____

_____

_____

_____

_____

_____

_____

_____

_____

_____

DAY 3: LET IT GO, LET IT GO!!!

"But forget all that— it is nothing compared to
what I am going to do."
Isaiah 43:18 (NLT)

---

*The truth is, unless you let go, unless you
forgive yourself, unless you forgive the
situation, unless you realize that the situation
is over, you cannot move forward.*
~Steve Maraboli

One of Disney's most popular movies features
a princess-turned-queen named Elsa. Elsa is a
beautiful girl with a chilling secret.

She's born with the power to create snow and
ice and can freeze things with a touch of her
hand. The only problem is, she struggles to
control her powers.

She hid her secret for many years, until one day,
her emotions overtake her and she inadvertently
reveals to the world what she had tried so
desperately to conceal. To make matters worse,
her actions have far-reaching, devastating
consequences.

She runs away, humiliated, and begins to sing the most famous song from the movie, "Let It Go":

Don't let them in,
Don't let them see
Be the good girl you always have to be
Conceal, don't feel,
Don't let them know
Well now they know

Let it go, let it go
Can't hold it back anymore
Let it go, let it go

Turn away and slam the door
I don't care
What they're going to say
Let the storm rage on.

The cold never bothered me anyway
It's funny how some distance
Makes everything seem small
And the fears that once controlled me
Can't get to me at all.[2]

With her secret out, Elsa finally realized that no matter what others thought, she had to live her life on her terms.

There's nothing more liberating than letting go of the need to live up to superficial standards,

19

standards that have nothing to do with who God created you to be.

Remember, God had a plan long before *they* ever had an opinion. We often hide our truth because we're afraid of how others will react. We end up living a lie, which benefits no one, least of all ourselves. We waste so much of our time paralyzed by fear and the opinions of others that we fail to truly live and blossom.

Today, make up in your mind to let go of anything that's not contributing to your growth. Choose faith over fear, and walk boldly in who you are.

What do I need to let go of?

DAY 4: ME VS. THEM

"Make a careful exploration of who you are
and the work you have been given, and then
sink yourself into that. Don't be impressed with
yourself. Don't compare yourself with others."
Galatians 6:4 (MSG)

Comparison is the thief of joy.
~Theodore Roosevelt

In today's digitally dependent and social-media- driven society, not comparing ourselves to others can be quite the challenge.

We have myriad social media apps with hundreds of filters and photo editing capabilities at our fingertips to help us post the perfect selfie.

After we've altered the original image to our satisfaction, we spend minutes, sometimes even hours, trying to compose a caption that will make the post relevant. We do all this to create a brand that we think will appeal to others.

In *I Don't Like My Life*, I say this about the relationship between our brand and our identity:

23

See, the thing is, your "brand" is just that. It's not your identity. There's a difference. Know the difference. You are more than clever captions, sepia-stained selfies, and tweet-worthy quotes.[3]

You, Beloved, are more than hearts and shares. You are a beautiful and unique creation of Jehovah God who holds the entire universe in His hands and He loves you beyond your comprehension.

When we spend our lives trying to create a perfect image, we say to God, "I'm not good enough and You aren't either because You made me..."

Deep, right?

Think about it. He created you just the way you are for a specific purpose. When we try to "fix" ourselves, we're telling Him, "Step aside. You don't know what You're doing."

Friend, we must realize that there is no such thing as perfection outside of Jesus Christ. Only He is perfect, and His qualifications are impeccable. There is no other like Him.

If perfection is your goal, realize that it is only in being uniquely you that you will ever realize it.

No one can be a better you than you. You have a distinct perspective to offer the world, formed by and filtered through your experiences.

Your experiences may not have been all good or everything you wanted them to be, but they were for your making.

They formed the fire that purified the goal inside of you. It was the pressure on the coals of life that developed you into the priceless, precious diamond that you are, and you can't be paralleled.

You've got the goods and no matter what they say, you are a winner.

Who would I be if I never encountered them?

DAY 5: CHARADES, FAÇADES, & MASQUERADES

"Thank you for making me so wonderfully complex! Your workmanship is marvelous—how well I know it."
Psalm 139:14 (NLT)

"Masks reveal. They don't conceal. Masks reveal your cravings, your passion, your deepest most secret desires." ~Chloe Thurlow

In the game of Charades, there's no talking. You pick or are assigned a topic that others must guess as you act it out. You offer as many clues as you can, using gestures, but not your voice.

Charades can be fun. It can also be a metaphor for how many of us go through life.

We pick out a perfect life and superficial reality, then spend a great deal of our lives buying into our own charade and trying to convince others of its truth.

So, we work to master our act, suppressing our true inner voice in the process, and then...*voila!* Our façade is complete.

A façade is an outward appearance maintained to conceal a less pleasant or creditable reality. When we give in to our charade, we believe we are covering something that shouldn't be seen or experienced by others.

We walk through life presenting everyone, most devastatingly ourselves, with the façade of who we think we should be or who we think they want or need us to be.

There's a beautiful song, "Stained Glass Masquerade," by Casting Crowns, one of my favorite groups. In it, the writer describes why we may behave this way:

So, I tuck it all away, like everything's okay
If I make them all believe it, maybe I'll believe it too
So, with a painted grin, I play the part again
So, everyone will see me the way that I see them[4]

For us, life becomes one huge masquerade ball where everyone wanders around with their faces covered, trying to be who and what they see around them.

Oh, the irony. When we try to imitate what we see in others, we often end up *imitating an imitation*. We merely mirror another person's cover-up.

You really don't know anyone, not even yourself. We know everyone's representative. We can only truly know the façade that they present. It is only in genuine relationship that we get to know people more deeply.

The point here is simple: don't get caught up in the cover-up.

After all, masks don't offer the protection we think they do. They reveal what they are intended to conceal...the very thing we do to keep ourselves hidden tells a lot about who we are, what we fear, what is painful, and what we desire.[4]

Be you. In all your flawed glory, be you.

What charades and façades are you committed to getting rid of?

_____

_____

_____

_____

_____

_____

_____

_____

_____

_____

_____

_____

_____

_____

_____

DAY 6: IDENTITY CRISIS

"⁴But God is so rich in mercy, and he loved us so much, ⁵that even though we were dead because of our sins, he gave us life when he raised Christ from the dead. (It is only by God's grace that you have been saved!) ⁶For he raised us from the dead along with Christ and seated us with him in the heavenly realms because we are united with Christ Jesus. ⁷So God can point to us in all future ages as examples of the incredible wealth of his grace and kindness toward us, as shown in all he has done for us who are united with Christ Jesus."

Ephesians 2:4–7 (NLT)

I'm a stranger in my own life. ~Lang Leav

Do you know you have a purpose? I'm sure you're familiar with Jeremiah 29:11, "For I know the plans I have for you," but do you *really* understand what that means. That God actually *does* have a plan just for you?

Here's what you may not know. The plans that He has for you are not even based on you. They're grounded in His grace, goodness, and glory. In the midst of your messed up, tripped out, and unbelievably difficult circumstance, He's still hard at work, using His grace to keep you, and your life to give Him glory.

Think about your worst moment in life. Go ahead. Take a few more seconds...

Got that picture in your mind now? ***God is getting glory out of that!***

Pardon the cliché, but it could have been worse. His grace was present with you even in that moment and you can tell someone about His sovereignty because of it.

The problem is that all too often, we get stuck in the place of *that*. We forget that there is life beyond *that*. We forget that we got over *that*. Well friend, I have amazing news for you. He died for *that!*

You don't have to own a stigma or wear a label assigned to you by someone else. You can live life unbothered by the condescending opinions of others. When you do, not only will you be fulfilled, but God will be glorified.

Allow me to reintroduce you to you. You are blessed! You are favored! You are anointed!

You are beautiful! You are loved! You are valuable! *You are enough!*

What or who have I given the power to name me? What do I need to change to reclaim my own power?

_____

_____

_____

_____

_____

_____

_____

_____

_____

_____

_____

_____

_____

_____

_____

DAY 7: THE STRUGGLE IS REAL

"[16]That is why we never give up. Though our bodies are dying, our spirits are being renewed every day. [17]For our present troubles are small and won't last very long. Yet they produce for us a glory that vastly outweighs them and will last forever! [18]So we don't look at the troubles we can see now; rather, we fix our gaze on things that cannot be seen. For the things, we see now will soon be gone, but the things we cannot see will last forever."
2 Corinthians 4:16–18 (NLT)

Perseverance is the hard work you do after you get tired of doing the hard work you already did.
~Newt Gingrich

Let's face it, life is hard. Yes, you read that right. I said, "Life. Is. Hard." Undesirable circumstances and situations—many of which we feel ill-equipped to handle—are unavoidable.

Yet, when you look back over your life and think about how you got to where you are today, oddly enough, you feel grateful for every experience because you realize that it shaped you into who you are.

When trouble hits, however, we are thinking no such thing!

We're often asking the infamous question, "Why?"

Now, I dare not have you think that you should be so holy as to look up during your suffering and declare, "Thank you Lord that all my bills are behind and I don't have any money to pay them..."

Or even, "Thank you Lord that my husband and all my kids are acting a fool..."

Instead, I encourage you to seek the lesson. You may think it's a little far-fetched to look for clarity during a trial, but stay with me just a little bit longer.

Every hard situation we face in life can elevate us to another place. There is meaning in everything we go through; however, we must be discerning enough to stick it out.

Remember, all that you endure has the potential to grow and advance you.

Paul said, "We are being renewed day by day and our troubles are small and won't last forever."

What you're going through has an expiration date. At the end of it all, you serve a God who is able to do more than you ever thought possible and has a good plan for your life that He will carry on until it's finished.

Today, write your prayers about things that you're concerned about or struggling with. Make sure to include the date. Then, watch God work.

DAY 8: IT'S NOT THEIR FAULT

"And forgive us our sins, as we have forgiven
those who sin against us."
Matthew 6:12 (NLT)

"O my people, trust in him at all times. Pour
out your heart to him, for God is our refuge…"
Psalm 62:8 (NLT)

---

*It hurts to let go, but sometimes it hurts more
to hold on.* ~Author Unknown

Have you ever found yourself saying, "If
_____ had never _____, it wouldn't be like
this"?

Maybe you've even thought, "If I could
_____ instead of _____, my life would be so
different."

Everyone has what my granny called *coulda,
shoulda, wouldas.* No matter who you are, you
can think of a way to fill in the preceding blanks.

But friend, let me help you: don't.

Regardless of what they did or didn't do, it's time to let it go.

It's time that you realize it's not their fault.

I know that's a hard truth and probably one you don't want to hear…but it's truth nonetheless.

They loved you the best way they knew how and did what they thought was best. Still, they managed to hurt you.

By design, you are a nurturer. You love deeply, freely, and unconditionally, so this hurt, it's problematic. You weren't prepared for the problems left in the wake of the pain they caused you.

That pain created emotional issues for you. Those issues, in and of themselves, weren't unhealthy, but left unaddressed, they became unhealthy.

Those unhealthy emotional issues explain why every person you date is fundamentally the same person with a different name. It's the go-to reasoning behind the belief that every woman looks for her dad in the men she dates. It's the reason some people just get stuck…

I like to refer to this as the I-Can't-Let-Go Virus, ICLG for short.

In the grand scheme of life, you must decide to forgive them, irrespective of what they did.

And let me help you right here. Forgiveness is not what we were taught as children. Forgiveness does not mean that you go to that person and announce that you forgive them, *yada yada yada*.

While at times this is apropos, true forgiveness is far from it.

Forgiveness is a process that occurs in your heart apart from them. Your forgiveness of them is between you and God. To forgive that person means to acknowledge the hurt that was caused and to move forward with the lesson that was learned.

It means that you ask God for a new heart toward them and still love purely even though you feel broken.

I'm not telling you to forgive and forget. I'm telling you to grow from the experience and refuse to continue to hold onto something that's hurting you.

I once heard it said that unforgiveness is like you drinking acid and expecting it to kill the other person.

Unforgiveness is one of those tricky little things that can instantly become a big thing. When we fail to forgive others, spiritually, we bring judgment on ourselves. Matthew 6:9 says, "Forgive us as we forgive others."

Think about it. If you aren't forgiving others, how can you expect God to forgive you?

Lest I lose my original point, it's not all about them.

You also have to forgive yourself.

Sometimes, the hardest thing about forgiving them is forgiving yourself. We scold ourselves because we feel responsible for allowing them to hurt us in the first place.

But today, walk in the freedom of knowing that it's okay. Life happens. People won't always live up to our expectations, BUT GOD. You have a God who loves you and is on your side. He's aware and concerned.

Pour out your heart to Him and forgive those who hurt you, especially if you're the one you need to forgive.

Today, write a letter to God forgiving them and you.

_____

_____

_____

_____

_____

_____

_____

_____

_____

_____

_____

_____

_____

_____

_____

_____

_____

_____

DAY 9: YOU'RE AN OVERCOMER

³³I have told you all this so that you may have peace in me. Here on earth you will have many trials and sorrows. But take heart, because I have overcome the world.
John 16:33 (NLT)

If you are faced with a mountain, you have several options. You can climb it and cross to the other side. You can go around it. You can dig under it. You can fly over it. You can blow it up. You can ignore it and pretend it's not there. You can turn around and go back the way you came. Or you can stay on the mountain and make it your home.
~Vera Nazarian

If no one ever tells you, please know, **you are an overcomer!**

Think about how far you've come in life…

For many of us, our stories aren't fantasies or fairytales.

Yes, some have been blessed with wonderful parents who would move heaven and hell for their sweet little angels...the ones who did everything right and had trust funds and other investment accounts setup in their kids' names.

If you fall in that category, God bless you and thank God that you have amazing parents.

But for those of us who don't, we have what I like to call a *Color Purple* Testimony... "All my life I had to fight..."

We've had to fight for everything!

Look back on those struggles today and rejoice. Celebrate your wins.

Look in the mirror and say, "You are a bad girl! You overcame the odds and you are amazing! You've played the hand you were dealt, went through the fire, and don't even smell like smoke!"

Today, *issa* praise party!

Take this day to be grateful for everything—the good, the bad, and the indifferent.

Make up your mind that you will do whatever you have to do to get to a place of peace, whether it's letting go of people or taking a break from social media.

You have too much invested in your life to neglect the treasure you have within. Relish your victory. Don't worry about tomorrow—tomorrow is bright!

Remember, no matter where you are, God is there and He has promised to complete the good work He began in you.

Make a list of everything you have overcome. Celebrate your victories!

_____

_____

_____

_____

_____

_____

_____

_____

_____

_____

_____

_____

_____

_____

_____

_____

_____

DAY 10: TIME TO ADJUST

"⁵Though good advice lies deep within the heart, a person with understanding will draw it out."
Proverbs 20:5 (NLT)

When I discover who I am, I'll be free.
~Ralph Ellison

Engage in a quick exercise with me. Take a few deep breaths.

Inhale slowly. Exhale slowly. Really focus on your breathing.

Inhale slowly. Exhale slowly.

Again.

Inhale slowly. Exhale slowly.

Calm your thoughts. Spend four or five minutes in this breathing cycle before continuing.

How do you feel? Relieved? Relaxed? Settled?

This next part may be slightly uncomfortable, but trust me it's so very worth it.

The fourth step in recovering from an addiction using the 12-Step Method is: *Make a searching and fearless written moral inventory of yourself.*

I believe this practice is important whether you're an addict or not.

I taught this principle in *I Don't Like My Life* and I think it bears repeating here. To conduct a self-inventory, you must:

Look at your life with powerful, penetrating, truth-exposing nerve. You ask yourself the deep questions, embrace the tough answers, and make the hard choices. You totally surrender to the process.

You evaluate how your beliefs, patterns of thinking, weaknesses, and go-to behaviors have led to unhealthy relationships and outcomes.

You think about the things and people in your life that trigger sadness, stress, anger, frustration, disillusionment, fear, shame, depression, or any other emotion blocking your joy and sense of purpose, and ask yourself what it is about these things or people that cause you to feel the way that you feel.

You think about the experiences you've had and the labels, opinions, and messages you've coopted as if they originated with you to begin with. You ask yourself how these factors have shaped your view of yourself, your life, men, women, money, God, kids, relationships, work—everything... and see if those paradigms, planted long ago in the soil of your psyche, are producing anything profitable, or if crap is cropping up everywhere.

Ask yourself if you're growing from what you learned or if it's time to plant some new seeds.[5]

There's only one rule...Whatever you uncover gets dealt with. There's no sweeping it under the rug or ignoring it; you must handle it head on.

In the journal entry that follows, you'll be faced with a hard question, one that I beg you to answer with as much honesty and vulnerability as possible.

The question is, "What's wrong with me?"

Resist the temptation to provide surface, socially acceptable answers. Avoid the superficial stuff like, "I need to lose weight."

I want you to really dig into the areas where real change is critical. Think about what drains you of your energy and drives you to do dumb stuff. List the things that you know you need to address.

Once you've made your list, take some time to pray over everything you wrote down.

You may not remember everything at once. If you think of something later, write some more. Do it as many times as you must. This is all about your growth.

There's no special gift for figuring it all out the first time or having the most concise list. The gift is in the growth.

"I will leave you with this: Feel what you have to feel, then deal with what you feel so that one day, you don't have to feel it anymore."[6]

What's wrong with me?

DAY 11: LET'S DO THE WORK

"If you are willing and obedient, you will eat
the best from the land…"
Isaiah 1:19 (NIV)

---

*Your visions will become clear only when you
can look into your own heart. Who looks
outside, dreams; who looks inside, awakes.*
~C. G. Jung

Okay, I know yesterday was tough. But just how tough was it? Did you uncover anything new?

Today, we'll take a lighter approach. The work won't be easy but it won't be as difficult as yesterday's assignment.

Review the self-inventory you created. If you were completely honest with yourself, then you listed one or more issues that you need to address.

So, let's do it. Let's take what you revealed and work with it. It's time to pick it apart, break it down, and trace it back to its source.

Perhaps you need to reevaluate the position certain things and people have in your life, and make some adjustments.

Take what you've learned and create actionable steps on how to begin the process of change.

Most goalsetting and self-growth advocates will tell you that your goals should be SMART:

- Specific
- Measurable
- Attainable
- Relevant
- Time-Specific

I'm going to suggest that you make SMARTER goals. So, your goals should be all of the above, plus, they should be:

- Evaluated Consistently
- Relished When Mastered

Your goals should be as specific as possible. If you don't specify exactly what you're going for, how will you ever know when or if you've made it?

Goals must be measurable. When you assign some form of measurement to a goal, it keeps you accountable and allows you to check your progress. Again, how will you know you've gotten there if you don't know where you are going?

Goals should always be attainable. In today's microwave society, we're often enticed by impracticable norms that compel us to reach for unrealistic goals. We spend too much time judging our 'year five' by their 'year twenty-five.'

Goals should be relevant. They should connect to where we want to go and who we want to become.

One thing that many of us fail to do with our goals is make them time-specific. You need goals that can be placed on a calendar and completed by a specific date.

It's not enough to say you want to read more. You should specify what you want to read, how often, and in what timeframe.

Goals need to be revisited often. Update them. If they no longer work or fit the purpose for which they were set, it's perfectly okay to adjust them to where you are and where you're planning to go.

There's no law that says that goals must be permanent. In fact, quite the opposite is true. They should be fluid and constantly evolving to serve you.

Last, rejoice when you've crushed your goals. Celebrate a job well done.

There are few things more gratifying than doing the work to complete a goal and being able to check it off your list. It's an amazing feeling to sit back and enjoy the fruit of your labor.

So, after saying all that, you may be wondering what your goals should look like. Here's an example:

Vague Goal: I want to lose weight.

SMART Goal: I want to lose ten pounds in one month.

SMARTER Goal: I want to lose ten pounds in one month. I will evaluate weekly to adjust as needed. As a reward for completing my goal, I will allow myself an ice cream cone.

Are you ready for some goalsetting? In today's journal, set three to five SMARTER goals. Remember, these aren't random ideas. You want to set goals that directly address the areas you identified in the previous journal entry.

Break each goal down into actionable steps. Keep your goals in front of you so you can review them often and adjust as necessary.

Create three to five SMARTER goals.

_____

_____

_____

_____

_____

_____

_____

_____

_____

_____

_____

_____

_____

_____

_____

_____

_____

_____

DAY 12: YOU'VE GOT THE GOODS

"⁵God is in the midst of her; she shall not be
moved; God will help her when morning
dawns."
Psalm 46:5 (ESV)

---

*The strength of a woman is not measured by
the impact that all her hardships in life have
had on her; but the strength of a woman is
measured by the extent of her refusal to allow
those hardships to dictate her and who she
becomes.* ~C. Joybell

Listen girl, I am so proud of you. You're still
hanging in there! Despite everything you've got
going on, you're still moving.

If you've ever had the opportunity to hear me
preach or teach, then you know one of my
favorite books of the Bible is Psalms.

In Psalms, you'll see David rejoicing one
minute and saying, "God kill all my enemies,"
the next. There's a Psalm for every single
emotion you'll experience on life's journey.

The specific Psalm we're looking at today is Psalm 46. It is a Psalm of celebration, penned after a victory against some evil foe of David's. While the Psalm sings of God's protection of Jerusalem, there are some principles relevant to your situation that I'd like to lift and share with you.

Psalm 46 expresses the idea that what happens around you is second only to what is in you.

In ancient times, city dwellers depended on nearby rivers for nourishment and transportation.

Jerusalem was a great and beautiful city; however, it had no river. What it did have, was God.

Jerusalem was home to the temple of God and the place where His spirit dwelt. Jerusalem didn't need a river because as long as they had God, they would survive.

What does this have to do with you?

There are many around you who seem to be in picture-perfect situations. You look at their lives and think of how fortunate they are.

Their story is not yours, and that's okay. Life comes with stuff we don't like and given half a chance, we certainly would have picked a different set of circumstances. But you have a secret weapon.

You have God on your side and He lives within you. Because you are His child, His special creation, His treasured possession, He's working on your behalf!

When you're feeling inadequate, I want you to remember something I shared in *I Don't Like My Life*:

You're worth loving. "For this is how God loved the world: He gave his "one and only Son, so that everyone who believes in him will not perish but have eternal life." (John 3:16, ISV)

You're worth giving up everything for. "Since he did not spare even his own Son but gave him up for us all, won't he also give us everything else?" (Romans 8:32)

You're worth living for. "And Christ lives within you, so even though your body will die because of sin, the Spirit gives you life because you have been made right with God. The Spirit of God, who raised Jesus from the dead, lives in you. And just as God raised Christ Jesus from the dead, he will give life to your mortal bodies by this same Spirit living within you. (Romans 8:10-11)

You're worth dying for. "But God showed his great love for us by sending Christ to die for us while we were still sinners." (Romans 5:8)

In short, you don't have to prove your worth; you're already worthy."[7]

Remember that God has made you for a purpose and you can and will withstand everything life throws at you.

Today, think about and list every positive quality in yourself and your life and celebrate them all.

Today, accentuate the positive. List every positive attribute about yourself and your life.

_____

_____

_____

_____

_____

_____

_____

_____

_____

_____

_____

_____

_____

_____

_____

_____

DAY 13: ROOM TO GROW

"28Are you tired? Worn out? Burned out on religion? Come to me. Get away with me and you'll recover your life. I'll show you how to take a real rest. 29Walk with me and work with me—watch how I do it. Learn the unforced rhythms of grace. I won't lay anything heavy or ill-fitting on you. 30Keep company with me and you'll learn to live freely and lightly."
Matthew 11:28–30 (The Message)

There are no 'ifs' in God's world. And no places that are safer than other places. The center of His will is our only safety—let us pray that we may always know it!
~Corrie ten Boom

We live in a nearly instant society. Everything is all about RIGHT NOW! We walk around with mini computers in our pockets, sometimes on our wrists. We no longer have to wait for information. We're constantly bombarded with pings, chirps, and vibrations, each bringing with it a byte of news that we probably could've done without.

One of the side effects of living in such a fast-paced society, however, is burnout.

It's not uncommon today for a person to experience burnout with education, work, family, and even God.

Societal pressure compels and cons us into trying to adapt to its norms of perfection.

We see life in filtered snapshots on Instagram, the number of likes on Facebook, or views on Snapchat. We're viewers of carefully curated timelines.

We don't see the fifteen pictures that weren't chosen, nor are we privy to the thirteen captions that got scrapped. We marvel at the manufactured materialism of others. Rarely do we experience the truth behind a given situation.

Even when things *are* what they seem, we don't realize that what we're looking at on our screens took years to achieve or amass.

Contentment is found in the rhythms of relationship with God. Over the years, I've spent a lot of time—and I do mean a lot—cultivating spiritual disciplines in my life.

Don't let that term scare you. You don't have to be a super-Christian to learn to cultivate or understand spiritual disciplines.

Here are three that have transformed my life that I believe will help you too:

Prayer
Prayer is an essential Christian practice—a building block of our faith. It is not some mystical activity where you're duty-bound to say just the right thing or use just the right words. Prayer is a conversation between you and God. You speak to Him as you would a close friend.

Bible Reading
The Bible is God's written Word. In it, there are messages, lessons, and solutions for every situation you may find yourself in as a believer.

While scriptures may not describe your situation exactly as it is, the underlying principles will get you to where you need to be.

The Word is our lifeline. The Word allows us to know God intimately and personally. Bible reading is not a complex process either, but it does require your commitment to seek Him through His word, dedicating what you learn to memory and heart.

For a better Bible reading experience, find a translation you understand. My favorites are the New American Standard Bible (NASB) and the New Living Translation (NLT).

If you don't own a Bible or would like to try out different translations, there are free apps available on nearly every operating system. Many of them include reading plans as well. Also, checkout the Rock City app, which has a Bible and reading plan that will read to you.

Journaling
The third discipline that has helped me tremendously is journaling. Journaling allows us to freely express our thoughts and feelings in a way that is open and fluid, without the judgment of others. I like to think of journaling as free therapy.

There are only two rules of journaling. The first one is easy.

Start. That's it. Put the pen to the page and write what comes to mind.

The second and final rule? Be consistent.

Consistency and willingness to spend time with yourself in the process is key.

I recommend journaling by hand. Something special happens when you use your hands to put your thoughts on paper. Writing activates special centers in your brain that instruct you to pay attention.

Ultimately, it's all about what you're committed to doing. If you prefer to journal digitally, no worries. There are apps for that too.

So, what should you write? Whatever you want. I prefer stream of consciousness journaling, which is considered one of the most effective forms of the practice, and for good reason.

Stream of consciousness journaling is when you write whatever comes to mind. There is no special formula or format to follow.

When I journal, I set a timer and allow my feelings to flow. I don't worry about spelling, grammar, or syntax. It doesn't even have to make sense. I just write.

When my time is up, I go back and read what I wrote and try to work through anything that sticks out. Stream of consciousness writing is all about clearing your mind and sorting through your thoughts.

Sometimes, I write prayers for myself, my family, and others.

I'm amazed when I go back and review them and see how God has moved. I feel stronger and have renewed wherewithal to continue the journey.

Other times, my journaling may be notes on what I hear God saying during my devotional time with Him.

And still other days, I write down what I've thought about during the day, or my reflections on the kind of day I've had. I record unexpected blessings or moments that made me unhappy. I even make lists of things I am thankful for. I close my journaling time with prayer. I commit my concerns and problems to him, and trust that His grace is sufficient and at work!

Irrespective of your journaling method or medium, get those thoughts out and give them to God.

One more thing. Your journal entries will look different at different points in your life. The end goal is the growth. Be kind to yourself and give yourself grace and room to grow.

Today, read Ephesians 1 and write about some of the gifts God has given you. Make a list of prayer requests and commit them all to Him.

_____

_____

_____

_____

_____

_____

_____

_____

_____

_____

_____

_____

_____

_____

_____

_____

_____

DAY 14: GET IN PURPOSE

But I have spared you for a purpose—to show
you my power and to spread my fame
throughout the earth.
Exodus 9:16 (NLT)

---

*To accomplish the purpose of God is to dwell
where his presence and glory is.* ~Sunday
Adelaja

The word 'purpose' is so overused and
misunderstood in today's Christianese that it's
lost its real meaning. Everyone's heard of it, a
lot of people are yapping about it, but very few
understand it and even fewer are living it.

God created every person with a specific
objective in mind. It's integral that you seek
Him to find out what that objective is because
that's where you'll find purpose.

Discovering our purpose isn't as hard as we've
made it out to be. We get so mired in the idea of
finding that one specific thing that we fail to
realize the ultimate purpose in life.

No matter what gifts God has given you or paths He leads you down, your ultimate purpose is to be a demonstration of the power of God.

Your story is proof that He is powerful. Think of your lowest point, your darkest hour, your worst day. Remember, God was in that situation with you too. It's the very reason you're still here.

No matter where you've been or what has happened to you, He's been there with you and has continued to help you through.

Maybe you've crystalized and concretized how to use the gifts God has given you. Or maybe you have questions and aren't quite sure.

Regardless of where you are in your journey, you're a reflection of God's glory. When you realize that you are a child of the Most High God, carrier of His name and of His glory, nothing can or will be able to stop you!

Today. spend some time thinking about your gifts and ask God how He desires to use you to spread His glory.

Make a list of your gifts. Pray that God would use them to make Himself known.

_____

_____

_____

_____

_____

_____

_____

_____

_____

_____

_____

_____

_____

_____

_____

_____

_____

DAY 15: PLEASE & THANK YOU

Be thankful in all circumstances, for this is
God's will for you who belong to Christ Jesus.
1 Thessalonians 5:18 (NLT)

---

*Do not spoil what you have by desiring what
you have not; remember that what you now
have was once among the things you only
hoped for.* ~Epicurus

We all desire something, whether it's to get
better, to get to the next level, to get paid; we all
want some type of growth.

Issues arise when we pursue these things at the
cost of what we already have.

In our quest for greatness, we often miss what
has been right in front of us the whole time. We
see only what we desire and miss the beauty and
majesty of the moment.

For example, I have five beautiful children. I
can remember certain things about the older two
that I don't remember about my middle son.
With the younger two, I know EVERYTHING.

But there were seasons where I was on such a quest to build certain areas of my life that I missed out on moments that I won't ever get back.

Now, while I will forever regret not being fully present in those times, I learned a valuable lesson: gratefulness.

I'm still building, but my goals have shifted. Ultimately, I aim to please God and take care of my family. In fact, I do everything I can to make sure that my wife and children are taken care of. I am now, however, much more mindful of and thankful for the time we get to spend together.

In my line of work, I see people at both their best and worst. Seeing struggle can help you appreciate the good. We are often keen on who left and what we lost, but we rarely take the time to thank God for what remains and who stayed.

You might assume it was easy for someone to leave, but do you ever think about what it cost someone to stay?

Today, make a list of everything you're thankful for. Once you begin to count your blessings, I promise it won't matter who left or why.

Today, read Ephesians 1 and write about some of the gifts God has given you. Make a list of prayer requests and commit it all to God in prayer.

_____

_____

_____

_____

_____

_____

_____

_____

_____

_____

_____

_____

_____

_____

_____

_____

DAY 16: IT'S NOT YOUR FIGHT

"Tell those who are terrified, "Be brave; don't be afraid. Your God will come with vengeance, with divine revenge. He will come and rescue you."
Isaiah 35:4 (GW)

You'll never do a whole lot unless you're brave enough to try. ~Dolly Parton

Life is scary.

We come into the world full of fear and anxiety. After being pushed and yanked, poked and prodded, we open our eyes to bright lights in an unfamiliar place to hands we don't know but have no choice but to trust.

It's downright terrifying.

Then, we must continue to navigate life dependent on people who we can't communicate with in a way that makes sense.

Yet somehow, we manage to get through.

Through our toddler years, adolescence, adulthood, and everything in between, we keep at it, doing the best we can with what we pick up along the way.

Life can be fraught with fear; however, there comes a point when we can embrace a difficult choice. We can choose to trust the God who is.

Now that may seem like an unintelligible statement, but roll with me for a second.

Our normal inclination is to fight to control everything, and though you may beg to differ, we're not in control of anything.

We plan every aspect of our lives as if we can actually control something. I suppose that's why we fight so much—because deep down, we believe that if we fight hard enough, we can determine the outcome.

We fight ourselves, our families, our friends...we even fight God. Until one day, we learn a well-kept secret.

We learn that our fight is with the enemy—the enemy who desires nothing more than to see us defeated. We fight against the power of the darkness, which apart from God, we are unprepared to handle. We fight an indomitable darkness that we cannot overcome unless we first surrender to God.

When we realize the beauty of surrendering to Him and letting Him handle it, a change comes over our lives and we are forever transformed.

When we submit to Him, fear becomes frivolous. We understand that it is He who fights for us. We remember that although it's not easy, He's greater. He's greater than *it*, He's greater than *us*, He's greater than it *all*!

There's a beautiful song by Contemporary Christian artist, Natalie Grant, titled "King of the World." It says:

I tried to fit you in the walls inside my mind
I try to keep you safely in between the lines
I try to put you in the box that I've designed
I try to pull you down so we are eye to eye
When did I forget that you've always been the king of the world?

I try to take life back right out of the hands of the king of the world
How could I make you so small?
When you're the one who holds it all
When did I forget that you've always been the king of the world[8]

Friend, take a moment to think about those words.

We spend so much of our time trying to prove that we *can* when He already *has*. We have to quit fighting against God and realize, He's on our side, He's always been in control, and He always will be.

List the fights you're letting go of.

_____

_____

_____

_____

_____

_____

_____

_____

_____

_____

_____

_____

_____

_____

_____

_____

_____

_____

DAY 17: YES, IS ALL YOU NEED

"⁸Say a quiet *yes* to God and he'll be there in no time. Quit dabbling in sin. Purify your inner life. Quit playing the field."
James 4:8 (MSG)

Safety comes in our nearness to God, not in our distance from our enemies.
~ Dillon Burroughs

Yesterday, we discussed the fact that we have a God who is able.

Today, I want to look at an even more sobering fact. We have a God who is willing.

In my first book, I discussed at length the difference between willingness and *wantingness*. Many of us want to change but very few are willing to do the work to change.

It's the same in our walk with God. We want to believe all the great things we've heard about Him, but few are willing to try Him for themselves.

God is not sadistic. When we draw near to Him, He will draw near to us. He is not playing a mystical game of Hide-and-Seek where He eludes us for kicks. His very desire is to be known of His people.

Get this. The entire reason that Jesus came into the world was to bridge the gap between a Holy God and a sinful people. Jesus came to fix what was broken.

When Adam and Eve sinned, it created a chasm between man and God that was only repairable with a perfect sacrifice. That sacrifice could and would only come through the blood of Jesus Christ.

Spend some time thinking of new ways to say yes to God and remembering the times you already did.

Write down some instances when you said yes to God and think of new ways to say yes today.

_____

_____

_____

_____

_____

_____

_____

_____

_____

_____

_____

_____

_____

_____

_____

_____

DAY 18: MAKE THE EXCHANGE

"Oh! Teach us to live well! Teach us to live
wisely and well!"
Psalm 90:12 (MSG)

---

*If you can't change your mind, you can't
change anything.* ~Orna Ross

"I don't know, I guess I'm just in my
feelings…"

How many times have you used that phrase or
heard someone else say it? A lot of times when
something bad happens to us we get stuck in our
heads, or much worse, in our feelings.

Ninety-five percent of the time—and I'm being
conservative—these feelings lead us to draw
improper conclusions. We find ourselves
feeling some type of way about something or
someone only to later realize—if we're mature
and working through our pain—our feelings
were based on faulty assumptions. We're angry
and confused based on what we conjured up in
our heads rather than truth and facts.

In Psalm 90:12, David gives us the key to life. All we have to do is to ask God to teach us to live well and live wisely.

The opening verses here remind us that life is short and our days are numbered. However, as believers, we should ask our gracious God to help us to have a heart of wisdom.

David is basically saying, "Look God, I know I'm jacked up and there's nothing I can do about it. Since I know it and You know it, please help me with my issues. I am bringing You my weakness. Can You give me Your strength instead?"

David shows us that the key to life is acknowledging our inadequacies and leaning into God to fix us where we are broken.

David shows us the power of changing our minds. If we change our thoughts to those of God, we learn to live life well and make the most of the time we have.

We're not bound by norms or what we've always believed.

If we seek our God who gives graciously, we can live a full life with all the blessings He promises and a life that we love!

Today, let's focus on making the exchange.

***In what areas would I like to exchange my
weakness for His strength? In what areas
would I like to live more wisely?***

_____

_____

_____

_____

_____

_____

_____

_____

_____

_____

_____

_____

_____

_____

_____

DAY 19: IT'S ALL IN HOW YOU SEE IT

"Yet what we suffer now is nothing compared
to the glory he will reveal to us later."
Romans 8:18 (NLT)

---

*The horror of Hell is an echo of the infinite
worth of God's glory.* ~John Piper

Problems in life are rarely fixed. All too often, it's our perspective that makes a situation a problem. Problems are opportunities, remember? (See Day 2 if you don't.)

When we view our experiences from a subjective point-of-view versus a spiritual point-of-view, we're left thinking, *What can I do to fix this? Why does this always happen? When will it get better?*

But when we realize that God is bigger than our problems and that He's in control, we learn to ask instead, *What's the lesson here?*

In every measure of suffering, there is a lesson that's meant to push us into a deeper relationship with God. Through these lessons, we come to understand something new about His character and His desires for us.

When we realize that everything we experience is a part of His plan, we learn to approach bad times differently.

It's easy to despise a situation and constantly complain when we're relying on our own power to fix it.

Of course, we're ticked off when our bills are behind and all we see is our limited bank accounts and paychecks.

But how differently would we feel if we realized that though our bills were behind for several months, God used that season to strengthen our communication and prayer time with our spouse?

It never feels good to suffer, even when we know that we brought it on ourselves.

But when we can put on our sanctified glasses and recognize that God is orchestrating every moment behind the scenes; when we know that He's working every detail so that not only will we get the victory out of our situation, but we'll grow deeper in Him; our thoughts just may change a little.

I'm challenging you to step back from your issues for just a moment and ask God to allow you to see your situation from His perspective. Ask Him to help you see Him at work and watch how your mind changes.

How have I seen God work in the past? How can I see Him working right now?

_____

_____

_____

_____

_____

_____

_____

_____

_____

_____

_____

_____

_____

_____

_____

_____

DAY 20: HE'S NOT DONE!

And I am certain that God, who began the
good work within you, will continue his work
until it is finally finished on the day when
Christ Jesus returns.
Philippians 1:6 (NLT)

---

*He started something good and I'm gonna
believe it. He started something good and He's
gonna complete it. So I'll celebrate the truth,
His work in me ain't through, I'm just
unfinished.*
~Mandisa, "Unfinished"

As we near the end of this journey together,
there's one thing I want you to realize: These
twenty-one days together are not the end!
You've seen Him work once and Beloved, be
prepared to see it again. That's the incredible
thing about our God.

You can't see it all right now, but know that
there are good things prepared for you, not
because of anything you've done, but because
of who He is.

He has started you on the path you're on for a purpose and He will carry it on until He is done. The best part about it is that you don't decide when He's done; He does.

Yes, you may get tired along the way and you may want to give up. That does not stop the work He's doing. He will continue to work in you. He will continue to grow and refine you.

No matter what it looks or feels like, look at your situation and remind yourself, it's not over. He's not done.

I remember when the devil thought He had one. Jesus was crucified, he died on the cross, and was buried. But three days later, He got up with all power, showing that He indeed was the Lamb of God.

You may be hurting and you may not like it but stand on your truth: Your God isn't done yet!

Remember Romans 8:28 in the NASB, "And we know that God causes all things to work together for good to those who love God, to those who are called according to *His* purpose."

Reflect on your life and write down situations that you realize are unfinished. Commit them to God in prayer.

_____

_____

_____

_____

_____

_____

_____

_____

_____

_____

_____

_____

_____

_____

_____

DAY 21: ENJOY THE JOURNEY

[10]Then the way you live will always honor and please the Lord, and your lives will produce every kind of good fruit. All the while, you will grow as you learn to know God better and better. [11]We also pray that you will be strengthened with all his glorious power so you will have all the endurance and patience you need. May you be filled with joy, [12]always thanking the Father. He has enabled you to share in the inheritance that belongs to his people, who live in the light."
Colossians 1:10–12 (NLT)

Too many of us are not living our dreams because we are living our fears. ~Les Brown

Friend, the last twenty-one days have been amazing! I pray that you have laughed, cried, reflected, and above all, I pray that you've grown. Don't see today as the end of something; view it as a beginning.

You've spent the last twenty-one days digging deeply into your life. Consider today a new start. It's the beginning of a journey with the knowledge of self and a God who is greater than any circumstance or situation.

Remember, life is an ongoing journey with ebbs and flows. Don't ever feel that you're stuck or too far gone to map out a new course. When things no longer seem to be working, dig your heels in a little deeper, try a little harder, or go another way altogether.

Fall in love with your journey. You deserve to love the life you live and live a life you love! After all, you only get one, and there's no one that can do life quite like you.

Walk around knowing that you can live your dreams if you're willing to allow God to silence your fears.

What have I learned in the last 21 days? How will I continue to grow moving forward?

ACKNOWLEDGEMENTS

To my wife JaQuetta, thank you for allowing me to not only dream, but to pursue that dream.

To my children whom I love with all my heart Xander, Michael III, Mason, Makinley, and Myles, know that Daddy loves you and everything I do I do with your future in mind.

To my father and mother, words can't express how much I love and thank you.

Dad, from moment I could walk and talk you've always told me that I was special and that God had big plans for my life. You gave me your stage, you allowed me to experience your wins and losses, all the while grooming and preparing me for my now. I've lived each moment trying to live up to the name you placed upon me, and I pray that I've made you proud.

To Rock City staff, I love you and I thank God for you. We've grown up together and through the highs and lows we've loved and supported each other in all that we've done. I pray God opens every door needed for you in this next season of our lives.

To Dr. and Lady Vernon, what more can I say that I haven't already? I love you and I thank you for all that you've been to JaQuetta and me. Thank you for your love and support. Seeing you guys interact, work together, and live for God motivated and inspired us on so many levels. From the bottom of my heart, thank you.

To Lesley Smedley, simply put, this book wouldn't have happened without you. You're a friend of my mind, and one of the most brilliant people I've ever met. Thank you for taking an idea and showing me how to write and connect with readers in a way that not just blesses them cognitively but heals them emotionally. This is the first of many.

Last, but certainly not least to Rock City Church. Everything I am is because of you guys. You loved me, allowed me to be myself, watched me grow and mature, cried with me, won and loss with me, and through it all supported my family and me. Without you there would be no me. I promise to do all I can to forever express the gratitude I feel and I can't wait to see what GOD does next.

Notes

1. McClure, Jr., Mike. *I Don't Like My Life: But I Love It.* Birmingham, AL 2017. p. 17.

2. Anderson-Lopez, Kristen, and Robert Lopez. *Let It Go.* Idina Menzel. 2013. Web. 30 June 2017.

3. McClure, Jr., Mike. *I Don't Like My Life: But I Love It.* Birmingham, AL 2017. p. 18.

4. Hall, Mark, and Nichole Nordeman. "Stained Glass Masquerade." *Lifesong.* Casting Crowns. Beach Street Records, 2005. MP3.

5. McClure, Jr., Mike. *I Don't Like My Life: But I Love It.* Birmingham, AL 2017. p. 48.

6. Ibid, p. 26.

7. Ibid, p. 11-12.